I0107493

Great Storms Making Ready

Great Storms Making Ready
Copyright ©2012 Stewart S. Warren

ISBN: 9780988227910
Publisher: Mercury HeartLink
Albuquerque, New Mexico
Printed in the United States of America

All rights reserved. This book, or sections of this book,
may not be reproduced or transmitted in any form without
permission from the author.

Permission is granted to educators to create copies of
individual poems for classroom or workshop assignments
with proper acknowledgment and credits.

Contact: stewart@heartlink.com

Mercury HeartLink
www.heartlink.com

Great Storms Making Ready

STEWART S. WARREN

THE POEMS

FIRST SET

SECOND SET

THIRD SET

FOURTH SET

FIFTH SET

FIRST SET

WOODPECKER WORK

A young woodpecker works at a branch,
his red Mohawk and dancing shirt
celebrating the triumph of bird.
As was done, is done again—

form fashioning form. The limb,
like his own body slender and lithe,
was only a practice piece.

The black mask pulled tight
across his eye
could be war paint,
which is also relationship.

Deeper still in the layered woods
his mate, quiet as gray bark,
poises for the next passing bug.

They're joined by insects that click and crawl,
by dove and warbler and wren,
by stalking cats and soft-eyed cows,
by the wind here then gone, by all

that extends the earth, that far flung idea
too deep in the ground to remember.
It is done, and done again.

A Rain Arrives

An afternoon rain arrives
   and trees, not just tossing,
      swoop low in urgent ellipses,
         West African dancers

gathering laughter in baskets.
   Children squeal. What began
      as a rivulet runs, gushes—
         torn leaves, exhausted lovers.

Do not say the word *storm*
   unless you mean business.
      Thunder rumbles around the city,
         a siren, a silence, a mind

thrown open, a stone cathedral
   of sudden coolness.
      Do you remember running
         for the barn; do you recall

newspapers swirling in the air?
   Everything inside you waits
      for lightning. This afternoon
         a joy arrives.

News from The Ice
a study of climate change

We waited for the ice, to witness
the night of regeneration.
We tethered our boat
against the glacial gale, wrote
our own epitaphs, burned them
into the sunless above.
The ice didn't come.

I mourned with penguins and seals.
I mourned in the garden of jellyfish.
I mourned with the puzzled plankton.
I mourned for the northern cities—Oh,
the dragon's tail of their exhaust.

Neither my obligation nor theirs
will bring the yellow moon around.
At the other pole pieces of her face
fall into the sea, a whale and pup
circle, circle without purpose.

Monk Mountain Stream

I know why he went deep
undercover, to the edge
of water moving, to the bank
where he was still, sitting
at the feet of saints.

He took comfort there,
the voice of stones washing,
the voice of the forgiving dove,
the mother of perpetuality,
a silence of sorts.
I know why.

But how much pushing away
it takes to make a clearing
in the woods is a division
that defies the perfected mind.
There's an ache in every forest.

He plays with his love
like it was something yet to come,
points it toward the spider on his leg,
toward chameleon clouds,
a lonely starless spot overhead.

Later he'll learn to bathe here.
Listening to water makes him thirsty.
I see how he's moving

closer to town. On a water planet
he finds the pulse strong
where two or more are gathered.
At sunset everyone comes to shore.

DISTURBED SKY

The screaming goes on forever.
In a pale quarter moon
the mother dive bombs;
the father circles, circles, circles.
Two demon eyes are caught
in a faulty flashlight, then
the crunching. The crunching.

Here's to all the abductions,
the abortions, the babies
fuzzy with fledgling feathers.
Here's to mothers.

We say gulls cry, but first
they howl, they wail.
They tear at the disturbed sky.
The ocean is not far,
but not close enough. The moon
is witness but not shelter.

In the morning the crows come
with their undertaker cloaks
and perfunctory trash hauler swagger.
They probably slept through the whole thing.
The raccoon licks fuzz from her face,
catches a nap undercover.

On another rooftop another mother
makes shorter trips,
keeps an eye on the sinking sun.
On a balcony across the courtyard
you install fresh batteries,
want to see the remains
of tiny wet bones, wonder
how the sky can hold another scar.

OPEN SPACE ECLIPSE
Albuquerque 2012

Scattered throughout the sandy knolls
a plethora of phlox, guara, yucca
and Apache plume bloomed
in the very late sun above the city.
Clumps of people in twos, fives and thirteens
clustered across the corrugated hills
and into the granite rocks
which are the beginning
of our mountain. Pilgrims,

I called them, and she
reminded us that for millennia
we've faced the same sun, yipped
and howled at these shamanic antics.

We must go inside, someone warned,
cover our heads, seek the darkness
of the hidden sun, become eclipsed.
What, I must wonder,
is all that shame about!

Shout deep down into the dark of it, shout
into our trauma and designer diseases, past
circumstance and configuration,
beyond our well bred reason.
Shout with a force that wants to know,
then—Stop.

And stopped we were,
star struck, as they say, before
that *Ring of Fire* framing the void, but
still in motion. The young ones who
do what we do and more
(and therefore are the wiser), have only
a passing curiosity about history and myth.
Spare us the stories, they say.

Standing before the eclipse
some sort of Sermon on the Mount
was delivered on high, was heard by all
who bloomed and ooh-ed and aah-ed
at the renewal of life on earth.
Our shadows blurred in sacred geometry.
On the walk back a young girl said,
I don't need the special glasses.

Hoop to Jump
Annular Eclipse of 2012

> *"Forget the dead you left, they will not follow you."*
> —Bob Dylan

The electricity is still on
but something like static
or fingertips fumbling for buttons.

Surges and spikes pulse
across the thought of heaven—images
   of the girls on stage,
   dream about the death of slam,
   Voyager flyby beeping deep,
   mother bird behind the scene.

From here the smallest and the largest of them,
Mercury and Jupiter, dance
a tight honeybee love
sooooo close to the sun.
Closer still, the moon.

Sharp angles arc, fish bark,
yesterday's menu turns to ash.
Say Goodbye, Goodbye, Goodbye.
The Ring of Fire has found you, jump
for your new life.

Pull of the Sea

The mist in the highlands has suddenly
pulled back, revealed
the white crash against dark rock,
the sea at sex with the coast.
You can smell it: the fish and salt of it,
the kelp floats gassing, the picked
and strewn shells, flies,
the roaring release of pure oxygen.
How were we to know?

Only by the gulls could we guess,
their squash colored beaks
stained with sunlight and crab.
Only by this profusion of flowers,
infinite hues of blue pointing
toward the arriving sky. Only
when we lowered our shields of disgust.

In our loneliness we gathered
the shiniest bobbles on the beach,
discarded the least until there were none.
Only when we faced the terribleness,
the immense lie, the smallness that must open.
An onshore breeze takes the fog
up, back to the sun.
Who comes here with empty hands?

Passed Through

I stared at Baboquivari Peak
    until it disappeared.
I drove to it. I drove into it.
Invisibility is not effort
but the absence of it.

I passed through Border Patrol checkpoints
    as nothing, nothing
seen, nothing believed.
Only the undulating plains
of sideoats and lovegrass raised
their spikelets in the wind.
The stars waved me through.

My old friend—Baboquivari,
they've placed their instruments
    beside you, hope to know
what you know. I will speak
with mountain lion about this.

On the other side
I reappear, a turn-of-the-century man
shuffling through shops in Old Town,
fingering quartz and copal,
touching nothing, not really
    there but here
in the familiar in between.
Your medicine is wide.

Here, On the Surface

You live in place where you can see
the sun to its final conclusion:
fireball, horizon, awesome exchange.
Be it last flash of green
or blink of burning pink, you feel
the mighty movement underfoot.
You stand on the earth.

Hear the hum of us
as we turn, leave the sun
to face it again. Hear the rumble
of cooling star beneath us,
the hiss and roar of magma
making new cities on ocean's floor,
our hot, dark, wet beginnings.

Ride the crust, this ship
across the cosmos, forward deck,
intricate tier brimming with forms.
Untold billions swim within you.
Everything wiggles.
Every sunrise a sunset, every thought
preparing the next bloom.

This is your home planet.
You live here, on the surface.

HIGH SUMMER BLUE

If you've been lonely
for a mountain or the slightest
whisper of a season
there is no hope
for you in this world.

Only half of me
is a herd animal,
and now the moon above
the city is not a comfort
but a tease.

It's high summer
but the sky leans two
invisible minutes a day
into the falling.
It knows dying

as the other side
of its own willing hand.
Down in Bosque Farms
they're getting a second cutting—
horse hay, sweet clover.

Two simple clouds post
above the Manzanos, a third
birthing in ether. The snow
will come from nowhere.
Not one leaf has turned.

THUNDERHEAD

A thunderhead stands next
to the mountain swallowing seeds,
dreams, hawks, whole airplanes,
the un-interpreted sky.

I return to the city, the most
fragile of the three, at the feet
of one, at the mercy of the other.
Not everyone here is fully human.

Or, not every upright
hears the ripple as music.
He wants dominion—and he'll have it.
My job is to love the earth

and treasure his inheritance.
He may join us later
in the finished star. It's true,
I love this city dearly. From here

I watch the turtle rise,
hear her singing to all the children.
From here I watch great storms
making ready, sweeping.

SECOND SET

Yellow

Across the newly flared horizon
geosynchronous satellites fall
from your semiprivate sky, heart wings flutter
at half mast, and though everyone
is talking at once only the quiet girl, only
the quiet girl with yellow purse,
is saying something.
You lean to hear her.

We stash the world somewhere
in our body; we pick up the pace;
we add and are added.
Shrines come and go, as they should.

The quiet girl with yellow purse
prays inaudible whispers
and a harpist dedicates his creation
to a waterfall in South America.
You think you catch a word.
Maybe *photosynthesis* or *sunrise*,
maybe *velveteen* or *deathmask*.

Maybe it was only her sighing.

A curve swings by and you hook up,
come out on the far side.
She introduces you to language
without symbol.
It's no longer yellow.

Celebrating the 4th

In the fourth world we were
on our way out. Where the canopy
of cottonwoods opened
    cloud people folded blue-gray
without rumble across early evening,
some sprinkles on old machinery.
In consort with cicadas
and darkening silhouettes a display
of Independence Day fireworks
flared in the distance.

From the east facing porch
of a gentrified bunkhouse we saw
the theatre of war, reenactments
of distraction, the buy-in trump card:
children frightened with sonics,
dazzled dumb by explosion. Nevertheless,

we went on with making art, the business
of bending light, the deconstruction
of story and remake of myth,
    riffs resonating on the scale
of our newly imagined humanity—
video, spoken word, flamenco guitar.
It's a good thing, she said,
when the guests stay to the end.

We were peasants at a wedding; we were
bathers running in the rain,
    horsetails to the wind,
impromptu apricot cakes.
We were the window
and both sides of the word.

Inside and out, candles took their time.
    We set our creations adrift.
In the morning: a stain
of gunpowder on the street,
pink clouds forming in currents,
    the new design
of who we might become
sailing, sailing
beyond the known.

CAPTIVES IN GRINGOLANDIA

Story is, she's in a cage.
Her husband Internet porns,
spreadsheets, rides the tractor
around the house.
Her lover pines on a string
over the hill while girlfriends
pass secret notes,
fan the bleeding flame.

At the coffee pull-through
it's that same blonde
car after car, replicants exercising
their freedom to choose condiments.
You can hold your phone
to the sky; you can pin yourself
on the page, but who dares say, I
don't have a fucking clue.

It all seems solid enough, you say—
besides, contempt is not the exit.
Something vibrates here,
but it's not my device.
The stars turn without it.

Anglo Saxon Zombie Conquest

Where, in your high science
and singular ownership of the day,
and now even the night,
will I find the trueness of blue?

You have gobbled the world
in continental bites, kept your blood
small, your lines pure like acid.
When, my grandfathers,
did you begin believing only in yourselves?
I am a Barbarian.

I have the papers to prove it, and papers
prove everything. You taught me that.

My blood is a sword;
my blood is a broken word;
my blood crawls
from sea to shining sea.
I am helpless in my armor.
I cannot touch you from here.

THE REINVENTION OF YOU

Sure, they're still building shopping malls.
You hear the clanging of it.
It's all prefab now, goes up
in a day or two. "Get your designer implants
right here." Ka-ching—
or is it a softer ringtone,
a green *ding* following the retina scan?
This is not an outside job.
I'm describing the landscape of your mind.

But even as you sleep some subliminal
rewiring is going on, the remake of you.
Behind us now: nothing, no going back.
You've read too much poetry, driven dangerously
close to the ditch, seen the manikins
flailing like broken toys
in the trash trucks before dawn.
You've swiped to a jailbroken screen.

An undercurrent is towing
the package you call you
into the depths where neon fish
cross the galaxy in nightly formations.
Others are here—not visible on prime time channels—
they're large and slow like overlapping moons.
You feel them when you look
past the outlines, when you let the shopping cart go.
I'm describing the reinvention of your mind.

One day some hardhats show up
with another blueprint, herbicide,
a privacy policy that looks like dialysis.
"Hey," you finally speak up,
"you don't have a permit to build here."

How Willingly We Go

It rolls over me, bone for cracking bone.
It catches me in its switching track,
attempts to sever my motion from hope.
It has circled the world.
    I have not stopped singing.

I am season's harvest, holding fast
to precious silence and ancient manners.
I am the author today.
Some value there was to turning myself
inside out; some brief comfort
in carrying the sign, having belonging
in the serendipitous magic of my time.
    Who will deliver the hero now?
The collective is blinded by its own sandstorm.

I have not run out of voices, they come
with each opening of the mind. As individual
as you wish, I speak for the moment.
Speak now — The wheel of the train
is taller than its industry, and the rubble
of us has built the grade.
You must lay its rails or fall by the side.
    How willingly we load their apps!

"At least," they sneer,
"you're not picking cotton, or lettuce."

It rolls over me, bone for cracking bone.
It catches me in its switching track,
attempts to sever my motion from hope.
It has circled the world.
    I have not stopped singing.

When It Matters

It matters which of my doors I leave open;
it doesn't matter on which street I live.
It matters that the rain has arrived;
it doesn't matter how we get wet.
It matters that we're in the boat together and
it matters that we sing. It matters to me
that a portion of joy has found you here.

It's none of their business where I go
but what I do matters in the way
a hatch of Mexican monarchs shifts
the course of distant stars.
It matters that you remember me,
but it matters more
that you see the moon in the water.

You're working it out for yourself,
for your family, for the village
as it tumbles through successive planets.
It matters that you keep your hands on the wheel.
It doesn't matter how many times
you think you've failed.
It matters what you choose to do
with power; it matters less
what you have between your legs.

Last night you called from a dream,
showed me some of your new work

from beyond the border. Everything
may, or may not, matter there.
Anyone that believes they're on their own
will fall through these lines.

It matters that matter forms;
it doesn't matter whether it sprouts wings or fins.
It matters that we pause at the sight of the sun
and it matters that you hold my hand.
It matters that we decide to make the crossing;
but in some hard-to-understand-way
it doesn't matter when.

As Agreed

What then is your survival:
avoiding the hooks
of consumer mind, that so called
sophistication of predator desire;
and where, now,
is your ancient mountain cave?
Here, I will sit for you.

I will sit for you in the rush hour
of your industry, the to and fro
of your making do, the surge of it.
I will sit for you as you crowd
along the water front,
the gun powder display reflected there,
the all night traffic jams.
I will sit for you.

I will sit for you amid
the road graders' growl,
the drone of drones,
the daily addition of personal channels.
I will sit for you out of harm's way.
I will sit for you.

I will sit for you in the flames
of libraries, in the flood
of senseless hate, the false
but pervading distinction of skin.

I will sit for you steady and still
in the deafening din, in the furnace
of the high rise, between the electric rails.
I will sit for you.

I will sit for you, a clear note
wide awake in the drowsy dirge
and drugged up sludge.
I will sit for you while the entertainment
of conquest falls and rises
and falls again, in the game show of politics,
the scurrying of fear.
I will sit for you.

I will sit for you here,
in the core of molten making,
in the cycle of rivers, the sandstorms
and charged particle waves, your
moment to moment misunderstandings.
I will sit for you in the rain,
in the strivings of your innocent heart.
I will sit for you.

I will sit for you though
you have forgotten my name.
I will sit for you as we agreed.
I will sit for you.

Past the Outer Orbits

The tired books have been swept
from the shelf; the open pit
of the moon opens wider
to give up more teeth; profiteers
design minds that want on command;
a little beauty breaks through.
You look like someone who could use
a hero or an all-night Laundromat.

You step aside, see a long line
of brothers pulling stones on a rope.
Glory to the temples of time.
It's tempting to have your own name
(and all the meaning you bring to that),
a holograph hovering in the empire.

She bears the water
up and down the line, her sister
cracks an electric whip.
But a cabin at the foot of Christ
or a farmhouse on the edge
won't change blood into wine.
This body was meant to be eaten.

How I appear to you is irrelevant.
The pixels of you are drifting.

THIRD SET

LISA'S SPRING ROLLS
and the sustainability of shared books

Driving back from The Projects
Bob commented that the sum of things we know
may only be about one hundred—
    that we know for sure.
That number seemed large
but I wasn't even sure
what counting was so I said,
My list is dwindling.
Traffic was sparse.

The streets weren't shiny so I didn't think
it had rained, but it might have,
shoulders of clouds leaned
    into the late city.
Conversation intermittent, we sailed
through intersections, paused at others.
The Book of Tea was written in 1906.

I had slept through half the reading.
On waking, ceremonial cups from Taiwan
like tulips, pert and empty,
nestled next to folded ebooks,
    and the line of our circle,
like ink in water, diffused
into the fugitive memory of night.

THE LIVING MUSEUM

I made a place to put them:
the long, low limestone falls where
I slithered from pool to pool;
the cockroach houses of the South leaning
under the weight of the moon;
the Missoula rain in my face
at a turn in mountain's road.
I bring my hand to the center
of my chest—Here, I have them.

People too: the star children
(of which I am one), the amphibians
and the so called walk-ins.
I have that moment of holding you
standing beside the car; I have wild
flowers all the way up the hill.
Each experience is some sort of grief,
which is to say, a joy.

Is it the earth that made my heart,
or is she the agent of this breaking?
    Even the stone corners of buildings,
    even the smart phone flat on the road,
    even the exhaust of rockets,
    even our tinkering with bugs.
I know now, I've been too hard on us.

Yesterday the moon passed in front of the sun.
I am a witness, not a landlord.
Out front, the street is growling.
Out back, the water's going bad.
It looks like this, *then*, it looks like that.
We'll grow whatever hands are needed.
I keep the old ones here
as a living record
of our love fumbling forward.

ELEVATOR MAN
May 25ᵗʰ, 2012

I sucked the last shots out of every bottle
in her house. Thirty years ago today
I couldn't get drunk, and that's
some seriously scary shit.

The elevator's on its way down, they say,
always on its way down. Get off now,
or try to get off later—
frayed cables, sputtering bulb.

Some switch had flipped, some trick
of chemistry, some diabolical betrayal,
some falling in the dark, going down
with my hands in my pockets.

This is just another trip
over a barbed wire fence story;
ripping my hand and bleeding
on her floor story; screeching brakes,
backing up, I'm sorry,

slamming doors, telephone harangue,
nobody understands me,
shrinking world story. This
is the inside of an elevator,

the going down part of the story.
"What it is, what it was,
what it always shall be." Man,
I was *so cool* in my little drop box.

Does that big red button
labeled "Emergency"
have anything to do with me?

My Greatest Asset

All those Texas miles: Lampasas,
Goldthwaite, Coleman, Abilene;
the pumpkins at Pumpkin,
the elevators at Adrian.
I drove them like pulling thread
in long tugs across the armadillo asphalt,
the hawk strewn skies
of the high plains and the cap rock.
I thought I'd stitch them together—
the Hill Country to the Sangres.

You can use your far-eyed vision to see
how the land wrinkles up
in a cetaceous seabed before falling for the gulf—
juniper, cypress, paintbrush, bluebonnets,
wet clouds rolling north.

I thought I'd sew my past into my future,
ride my sobriety
on the limestone filtered waters
of Barton Creek and the San Marcos,
on those hot recovery rooms
where the hard-earned light burst through.
Moving on, I thought, but not goodbye.

Some bridges buckle on their own;
some threads don't hold.
After while my trips to Austin were

fewer and farther between; after while
memories are a poem, a bookmark in a book
opened every other birthday.
But my awakening was not a sudden
and spectacular upheaval—my love
is of the educational variety.
You know what I mean.

Mountain bluebirds migrate
across the high ripping grass
and I can only guess at the rain
sweeping down through Central Texas.
The live oaks there change leaves
according to their own season; life,
it seems, is not a self-help program.
Fare thee well, after all, is what I came to say.
I'm throwing my sword into the lake, turning
toward the mountain, leaving my story
to hover in the wind. The little I know
is on the tip of my tongue.

"Slackers"

Drinking (for those of us willing to do the work)
went like this: bring yourself up
even with everyone else
by slamming shots *before* the party,
insist on driving, help the slackers
by finishing their bottles, then—
if your continued good luck lines up the cards—
the body will render the mind unconscious
just before you ingest that final and fatal ounce.
Life's a gamble.

Blackout: it's a kind of failsafe you bet on
like someone turning off the lights
just before you reach for the gun.

But hangovers are the real death;
long, torturous, bewildering.
At two in the afternoon I'd crawl
down the hall, pull myself up
to the lavatory, put my mouth under the faucet
and begin the process of hydration.
Hey, we all have our daily rituals.

If drunks are going to provide do-gooders
with excitement, training and purpose
someone has got to be willing,
by god, to do the work.

DRENCHED

As we made the intersection you said,
They're the same—life and death.
Green, red and amber lights winked
in every direction, coming and going
according to so called contract.
We sailed through, your shiny red Jeep
just out of the carwash tunnel, groceries,
technology, snacks for the city.

From a sidewalk restaurant we watched
children and white shafts of light play
in the intermittent but well-timed
gushes of water shot straight up
from a public fountain.

Fathers with toddlers on shoulders
raced across the tiles, betting
against the odds of sudden geysers.
Teenagers brimmed, nudged one another
at the edge. Oh, how we flirt with it.

The waitress brought strawberries and tea;
the outdoor music made the movie.
Someone has to live this life, you said.
Diners under umbrellas
not-so-secretly wished to get drenched.
The busser winked.
I felt some water on my cheek.

At a Reading the Thought of You
for Carla

Whatever the poet said I wanted
to bust out, to break from the bookstore,
run into the street, the last light
of summer against the mountain,
the last words of trust and blood.
She spoke of women
in the 60's, the political act
of their secret love,
their anonymity fading on the page.
I wanted to fly from the room,
go to you, a woman
with stepped-on feet—the last woman.

Sor Juana wrote in code,
signed her confession in blood,
dreamed under her dress, bloomed
as a night flower in her sunless cell.
The poet spoke for the voiceless architects
of the revolution, named
the nameless, those without papers.
Every line gave me reason
to fly. The bird in my chest
turned toward the home of us.

Cuba, New York, the coast of Argentina,
lovers who swear to stay forever, the brevity
of all forever's. I could hardly breathe.

Titles from spines leaned from shelves,
lives opened, quivered
in print where the impossible takes a chance.
I wanted out; I wanted in;
I wanted your body in which I could expand,
could shout in a whisper
that only you
would know, would understand.

The people at the reading
were listening; the people
were luminous as human beings,
were wired to the frame
of wonder, tethered
to tragedy and sad waterfalls.
I loved them, a field of poppies
rimmed in light, every orange cup
lifted toward you. I was out
of my body; I was out of my mind.
The poet read on.

Your name was
the sunset, the brilliance,
the loss of everything.
I cannot die here, I said.
Every poem reached for your face.
I told myself
you are not really far away.
The sun cannot be stopped
from dropping into the sea.
Most of me has flown.

At Chimayo It's the Water

They come for the dirt, something they thought
got rediscovered in this country of conquest.
Elsewhere it's water they want,
some tangible light to put on their forehead
or in the pocket of their heart. They come
half way around the world to see her weep.
When they cry—she cries.

At the beginning of summer we held hands
in that dirt. The Santuario was empty, resting
after another day of letting pilgrims
touch her garment and shuffle past her brother.
I reached through the sand to find you.
I heard a sigh. Was it the silent bell of an exhale,
or sad children in the saints' hall of fame?
I felt her gaze. How could we know

what lie ahead; a journey is just that—
a dance with the unknown.
So we touched, the holy dirt slipping through
our fingers, while the world in the next room
thumbed through instructions on annihilation.
Red candles strained in racks, sheep leaned against the fence,
the priest snored in his office.
We had the place to ourselves.

Are you afraid? you asked.   Yes.
Then we are real and only her weeping
can save us. In the courtyard,
pigeons were coming home;
in the village streets, not even a dog.
A few bees lingered in white Catalpa blooms.
The Chapel of the Santo Niño was closed.

We left with the late afternoon sun, followed
the Santa Clara into the mystery of love.
We were on our own beside a river of tears.
As far as we could see—
the junipered hills and heaved up orange dirt.
As far as we knew—only the angel fire sky.

BLOOD SUN CANDLE

Today I learned
   there's iron in our sun,
     a mineral only

a second generation star can know.
   We've each been married
     before. We've been buried.

Layers of rust and crystal and salt.
   We know the hard core
     of the earth, the need to breathe.

Help me not be afraid
   of my past, of yours.
     We're walking together

in the onyx mines of Mexico,
   so much exposed now,
     so much still in mystery.

A lover's moon pulls us back
   and forth, sea to desert, together
     then apart—the tectonics of us.

The sun is in our blood.
   Oh, our tempered hearts,
     our carnelian flame.

Star Welder

Mowed and raked and giving again,
the fields of the Estancia don't question
the hands that turn them.

Late summer has scattered a sigh
of green and gold across
the antediluvian expanse, a place
some call the journey of death.
We gave them succor
and maps to their imagined gold.
You can hear the thirsty axels
cry at night far out on the Interstate,
but we don't go there,
lest we have to.

I'm still pulling scones, says Mary,
a star on her forehead
and one in her walk.
How about some
kicked up comfort food
and a little local news?
I'd run her for congress
but she and her man are doing
all the good right here
in Mountainair. You can't tell me
there's no love left.

She learns the secret

of bringing children: something there is
that's trustworthy, that sends the sap
up and down the sugar of it—
little to control, little need to.
     Remind them of all the good
     they've ever done, then send them
     sailing through that great window.
When it's time to participate
in disaster a notice will arrive,
a coyote or crow, a cancer cell,
a call from long ago.
This won't be the last hard rain.

Twisted by the wind and growing
through the cracks, he welds
sunflowers from 1" pipe.
Did I remember to say,
they grow artists here?
Leroy takes me out front,
shows me the sign:
What a Star — You Are.

There's a cross here. It's not religious,
but the intersection
of the physical and spirit. Look,
he says, a dragon in the subconscious,
the hiding place of fear.
His ancient archetype is made
of metal flowers:
preacher in the pulpit nostrils,
hibiscus eyes, morning glory ears.

Those war mongers
can't hook you when you know
what demons are made of.

In the space of time it takes,
the purple mountain pulls the rain to it.
I sail between, between
this oncoming good
and the deep need of it.

I wave at the east/west train.
I wave at the high dark rain.
I wave in my sleep at the star
above your bed, that presence
you could turn to.

WHERE TO LOOK

I know where to find the outlaws—
down south and skinny as Ocotillo, or
on the faded pages of cheaply pressed books.
I know the song of rattlers
    denning under singlewides.
I've followed some falling stars.

And I've been through Iowa in the summer
where they factory the tender corn, cast
shame on misplaced commas.
I saw them from a distance.

What women know is not where
the wind blows, but how
the roots touch deep in the dark
of successive abductions and solar yearning.
I can only touch the skin
    of their wisdom, their immense wisdom
torn from history at Nicaea,
their birthday wishes lost
in the din and blood bath of war.
I want everyone to have a baby.

He stared at the stars until
he thought he moved them. I know
the "I am" at many levels.

In the middle of the day I found
a rattle snake coiled at the base of a sage.
I knew to look there. Seeing
was sufficient. One day
    you'll see me
blooming brilliant as Ocotillo.

MY PLACE IN TOWN

I saw the ripples then, the shimmering
of the world, the warriors
in their places, the intricate designs,
the trampled flowers at the edge of the road.
I saw how you mean to mean well.
I heard you then.

I told my story up and down,
hung strips of flesh, pounded
the earth with both fists,
tried to hold the door for others.
We can take those shrines down now.
The clouds have come close;
they dance among the trees.
I wake in leaves, hear the moon coming,
tribal drumming in the center of town.

If someone wants to know I'll tell them
how the planets wave in the wind,
how precious is their brief time without end.
Today I'm glad to be a worker.

Show me the hammer and chisel,
where to stand among the scattered chips.
I could fall in love with friends.
You'd have me back, my quiet return.
Some ringing of stone, this
momentary pair of extra hands.

FOURTH SET

CALIFORNIA ON THE HORIZON
(thunderheads crossing the great divide)

I am returned to white rock.
I am returned to steep slopes
of yellow earth and wide grass skirts
where the sea builds
and chews at dark mud.
I am returned to your fragile hem
and dignified red forest.
Shy, I am returned.

The desert of rainbow dirt,
already at my back, never rejected me
nor ever told me lies.
It's ultraviolet dose
kept my appetite clean.

The line of it, that is always
a circle, knows me like wire and wind,
clouds, no clouds, stars on the ground.
I was finished in its gaze.
I was never done.

And now, returned
to water-without-end,
the ancestors behind me,
the tall walking rain.
It may have all been a dream.
The salt up ahead is alive.

In the City I Wash My Hands
reflection on a difficult migration

I arrived in the city a refugee, lost
for words and missing
the modular body parts
of a snap-on society, a bit shaky
but willing one more time.
I snuck in under cover of busy day
brushing out the blood in my tracks,
still quivering in the hollow air
of the remote north, the dark-knife-side
of Shinning Stone Mountain.
I was not entirely empty.

The iron in my blood had kept turning me
toward a north that seemed
false or too far away.
Had I failed the neighborhood,
the foster family of brown, the pale white
earth sinking into darkest red?
I knew better. . .
the teachers had told me
that this valley belongs to no one,
just like the rest of my planet body.

The current configuration of campers
on the shoulder of Pedernal
chased me away under a flag of shame.
Love, after all, was not the local language.

I admitted my hands were not clean
and they showed me a bucket
of rusty nails, a hammer. Finally I said,
I've had too many turns in the barrel.

The Apache, the Ute, the Diné, the King,
the Black Robes and the White—no one
will own *this* valley. No one.
The quick silver of my heart's learning
had touched me down, then
snatched me back into the sky of my moving,
orphaned again, holding only
the song of it.

WOODSIDE, UTAH
a notebook sketch

The stage came through following
the base of the Book Cliffs, rutting its way
up through smaller bluffs, then
the narrow gauge, that scavenger
feeding on wood, coal and water,
shooting elevations, cutting grades,
hooting and screaming far into the salt.
Then the old road, then the new—
gasoline, rubber, onlookers.

I wrestled the pickup over dunes and down
the hard sand to water's edge. The tailgate
creaked and popped when it dropped.
I hauled 'em—bucket after bucket in the desert.
The 55 gal. drum sloshed on my way back up;
the horses curled their lips; the pigs
got the last of everything.

I'd look at the squat cabin and I'd look out
across the shimmering flats, and I'd wonder
how far the old timers had to drag those timbers.
I'd wonder about Abby rangering
just south of there, looking through red
sandstone windows, framing the same stars
in delicate arches. And I'd wonder
what I would've done if that bull snake
curled on my bed had been a rattler.

I worked for Red, the color of his Pomade hair,
the color of his round flat face.
He had a flaw that ran through the handle:
he thought polygamy included his daughters.
I lasted three and a half weeks, then
hit the road after hearing that.

The good people who tended the geyser
and gas station at Woodside pulled folding money
from their jar and stuffed some in my pocket.
I left with a western shirt and jeans bought
down in Green River and rolled up
in a Navajo saddle blanket synched with leather,
slung over my shoulder. I helped out
wherever I could. I stayed under the wire.
In the Northwest where I wandered next, the water
in grand cascades dove over the mountains.

NORTH NORTHWEST
for Tani Arness

At the mouth of the river
I felt the pelting rain
as it swept in from the sea,
smelled the pulp simmering in sulfur,
heard the saws, the jaws,
the chokers winding on a reel.
I heard the women say
what women say, and the men
say in their quick-coupling way.
I stood there—on the Pacific Rim.

Did I bring to each new woman
the accumulated loneliness
of all those that went before, or
a stand of bamboo, stronger,
taller, bending with the wind?
The glacial till of the softer coast
and the dunes with their running succulents
lay low between the fresh and the salt,
invited all to the green.

When the clouds broke, her skirt waved bright,
her strong arms and steel-eyed look
unfolding the day to dry in moment's sun.
I helped her at the chopping block,
and I stayed out her way.

Poets and other artists surrounded me
but I didn't know them
by any appointed badge. We were all
as famous as it really gets.
Nobody gave a shit.
I think some of them went on.

When it was time for Canada
I sold the Studebaker station wagon
for seventy eight bucks to the neighborhood.
    The ravens and the gulls,
    the surf against the hull,
    the passages too narrow
    for southern pomp and idle worship.
I stood on the prow, my face
forward in the fog.
I felt the horns as they reached into it.
Already St. Helen and the Columbia
far below, far behind. Already
that woman with smoke in her hair.

THE TREE THAT HOLDS UP THE WORLD

Coming then going across Garrapata Bridge
we looked for *Yggdrasil.*
We hugged the steepness
of the Carmel Range, memories
of fog and failed ventures dissipating
in the seagull updraft, a nap
of crimson/orange ice plants climbing.

A thin tide line of foam lay
in a curve on the water
as if cast by the moon—then kelp,
then rushing waves, then curling sand,
then rocks and birthing pools. Everything
happening in layers.
The coast highway too, a fine line allowed.

The legend of *Yggdrasil* has roots
somewhere on this road. A story
of metal welding and stone carving,
of high winds and helicopter installation;
a story of chiseling and marble chips
in a sculptors yard across from Cannery Row.

But the nine worlds of the Norse
are also grounded here: the nurturing,
the wisdom, and the terribleness
that keep all, for this moment, from falling

back into the night sea.
We carve this tree again and again.

We carve the story so you'll
remember. Children, you come from
the depths of breath breathing, the bird
within the snake, the eye of the fire.
Your ancestors are great, and are living.
On every hill we left a mark of the wind.

Lift the stone into the sky.
Say these ancient words in your own
new tongue; find the trees and feed them.
Iron and stone and wood may burn,
may fall into the ocean.
Where you step the sky begins to dream.

Carmel by the Sea

When the fog is in, the trees
are close: madrone, eucalyptus,
coastal pines. You can feel
the shaggy bark,
moss rock, textures of sky.

A gull curves close;
you eye one another.
The moment is gone in a glide.

High-winged cypress fade, slip
from this reality into another—
one limb in, one limb out,
they are enveloped; they are
ghosts, they are gone.
Beyond the secret mist:

a suspicion of sea,
that great being delivering
fog across the theater
of her upturned face.
You don't know
what goes on there.

You are allowed two or maybe
three streets, a galaxy
of cool blue hydrangeas,
a stir of wind,

distant horn, damp clank.
You wonder when your feelings
will come into view.

Is that some sadness
beyond the last wet rock,
or perhaps a wayfaring joy
waiting to come ashore?
Smaller birds turn
in and out of it.

FISHERMAN'S WHARF

jellyfish, jellyfish, jellyfish
   crab

jellyfish, jellyfish, jellyfish
   seagull

jellyfish, jellyfish, jellyfish

sea lion—*arf, arf, arf*

pterodactyl shadow
   pelican

toy poodle
   huh?

The Stanislaus through the Sierra Madre

Mountain upon mountain
of deepest green, tallest red,
azure beyond words.
The massive white rock itself
is a star humming low.

Your thoughts are lost
in magnitude.
You must admit something here.

Above the falls silence is not an absence
so you lean into a redwood or cedar
and remember what it means
to be a niece or nephew or
a thought not fully formed.
You are small,
and that is a comfort.
A red tail teases above you.

Summer is at its height; in everything
a hint of whitest winter.

You follow the waters out
toward familiar golden hills.
You move with it.

Time in Lake Tahoe

Boats rock in their births; Scorpio
dips its tail into the lake; other lights
appear on the horizon of ancient water
        and are nestled
into pleats of faraway pines.

The wind that was strong
in the afternoon has spent its bloom
along with evening's fuchsia smudge.
The only red at this distance
is Saturn and the port side
of a fishing boat returning
late for dinner, or bringing it.
We ride the waves of nostalgia.

The sweet bouquet of the *pina bete*
sparkles in the nose like gold dust
and ginger, sugar almost burnt,
        a shall of perfume wrapping
around the shoulders of all that stands.

We stand on the shore and cannot
do other than face the center.
Our past began with these gray rocks.
And now we can barely recall
        our own fleeting steps,
and the smooth stones are cordially quiet.

All the lights eventually die
into the dark cinder cone
of the long forgotten. The fantasy is
that we have been left behind
or have not yet arrived.
At the end of the pier something
you call your future begins—
      the unfathomable depths,
      the unseen stars,
      the certainty of loss,
the captain tossing a rope.

HABOOB

At Phoenix we're just in time
for a dust storm. Air conditioned
and behind tinted glass
we watch the world roll up in a wall.
It's 109°.
A Boeing 737 dropped me off
a half hour ago.
I'm not late to any *where*.

Whatever has made my life
of interest to you was happenstance
and may have gone unnoticed by me—
an offhand comment, a plane crash,
a reference to a shelf in your heart.

The man by the window announced
that he just wrote the book
that Einstein couldn't; something
about the unification of everything.
I mean *everything*.
He said people were stealing his work.
I said, Good luck.

Wingtips and tailfins come and go
in the moveable desert.
Jockeys on tarmac wear goggles.
When I get above 10,000 feet
I'll text you the outcome of this.

Until then, piercing headlights descend
through three dimensions
of computer generated space.
I could bring them all down
with my phone.

We're delayed. . . substitute planes
are being brought in.
I may slip out for awhile,
find an unattended body
on Concourse B en route
to Montreal or Rio, climb aboard.
I've got a few comments about unification too,
and if they're real,
stealing is impossible.

ONCE A RAMBLIN' MAN

I had a bottle in my boot
curved against my skinny shin.
I had the fire.
I had the highway.
I watched the rain from under the eve.

The Hippies came through
with their caravans, their paint
and homeless marriages; then
some old hobos slinking,
the constantly accused,
a temporary Christian with a banjo.
I slipped right through.

I was more invisible than most.
My harp didn't get stolen
like guitars did. I kept
the important things close:
family shame, artist's eye,
the neediness of skin,
my contract with the wind.

I was never lost,
nor without a tune. A hotel room
was the backseat of a Dodge with overdrive.
I slept through gulf coast fog.
In Idaho I used my boots as a pillow,

but the stars, the stars
kept waking me when they hit the ground.

I was even more afraid of girls
than I am now—I couldn't seem
to give either of us a chance
but I almost wrecked a few. I'm not proud.

And I'm not quite done with that dream
about the dirt lane
that crosses over the tracks,
but I'll leave conclusions
to the middle aged.
I'm just saying
there's a weather-beat house still standing,
ash and oak crisscrossed overhead,
the peoples' music rockin' inside.
All down through this overworked country
we're making our way to it.

We Are the Drum

Who speaks for this night:
the resonate wood of the deck hanging
off the east end of the old house;
string of starlet lights wound
around the rail; dancing candles;
chairs in something like a circle?

We drummed down the sun,
Rosario said, and the moon
rose in balance. Suzanne
gathered wheat and waves
from the earth, pushed them
with her mother-making
into sky's oncoming flower.

We fell into the groove
with wood and metal and living skin.
We invoked. We thanked.
Shango arrived, some neighbors,
travellers, the evening star.

We made music by listening. . .
    the hum of ancestor trees,
    night silence of chickens,
    children in the center,
    drone of summer bugs,
the bell——bell bell——bell.

We put our hands on skin.
We played our hearts
until there was one.

FIFTH SET

CRY ACROSS THE MIST

Highway, mountain, curse, dream.
Go ahead, utter the word *water* aloud.

Repetition is searching, random
variation is a star with dorsal fins.
Every million or so a new finger appears.
This is where we find ourselves:
a thought considering its mommy,
a heart wondering if others are here.

Go ahead, the water holds you.
Your head is already covered
by the blue shall of sky.
You hold the knife in your paw—
bread or blood, one or other.
I flower here in the center because

I flower here in the center.
Go ahead, say but the word.

THISTLE
for Rona Fisher and her grand adventure

They'll tell you about our
many migrations, how we followed
the edge of the ice, then crossed
the water to step upon the stone.
You'll remember the names
given: Alba, Caledonia, Scotland.
But who dares
name the spirit of it?

In my dream I am
the massif rock rising
above the swell of the sea,
the loam and peat at my feet,
a crown of higher stone
teasing with hawks. I am
the north wind, fierce
in my love of this stormy coast.

They'll use the word *ancient*
as if to understand me,
but you've entered *my* world,
not the other way around.

I dream this land walking,
staff in hand,
with all the children in me.
Great strides I'm taking

but not as a conqueror—Oh,
they fancy they've done that,
but the Stone of Destiny
is the very land you're walking upon.
All creatures are guest to it.

And if you've the heart,
travel deep into the narrow of it,
into the loch of it,
the steep and sloping,
the cry across the mist.
Of this, I shall say no more;
where the North Road ends
your dream begins.

DRESSING FOR THE DAY

I am held in the smell of summer's city,
morning breeze tickling leaves,
sunlight's song tapping
green notes on its way down.
I extend my hand to catch it.

I am quaking. My name
is a tone under and over,
seeking to be in accord.

You come to me as bitter metal,
pungent geranium, sweet roses
and corn; as sweat from shops
and old lumber, as peaches.
You come to me as diesel.

You come to me as half-used cans
of oil based paint, as
peanut butter and jelly kisses.
I am hungry for this music.

I breathe you in, deep
below the navel, above the crown.
This clear ringing
I wear into the world.

IN MY BUILDING A WOMAN

In my building a woman
is singing on the stairs—
Swedish or Gaelic or lavender.
She is often disguised as a conifer
and I pass without speaking, yet

her sweet and resinous breath
is the deep green
of everything I hope.
Like that—she's gone.
Like that—she arrives.

This morning her small tune
lilts and dances
as she descends. Last night
her face was so black
I fell awe first into Ashé, Ashé.

I won't burden her with my failures;
she can see that I'm trying.
She hears the whimpers of the chainsaw.

Something Like a Wormhole or Deliverance

You cross the street and it's done,
not even a curb. Was there
traffic to dodge?—doesn't matter.
The new view has less things:
a café with rounded corners,
a sky when needed, a spoon
when called for.
More quiet than what?

Elsewhen there was scrambling,
something you made up:
bumping, phoning, shooting in the dark,
a lot where they covet cars
and take the howling train.
You could wave to them. You could
wave your arms all day,
but they pass in a dream.

They closed their doors
but didn't go inside. It's true,
your invitations were a bit overdone
and signing in secret invisible ink
probably didn't help.
Whatever they thought they desired
they saw in you, but it all happened
back there, back when,
on the other side of the street.

It's not a question of following.
Love can't be unrequited.

So kick back in the café, have a bowl.
Someone will invite you to the sea—
a shell path, wooden stairs down
to the beach, the swallowing roar,
the longing you thought
was your own
coming for you, as they say,
out of the blue.

THREAD

And though I've not opened a poem
with death, I'll wait this time
to introduce those trees or line of land.
And though, as we know,
there is no such thing as waiting,
I'll come round about
in my way of saying the end.
Isn't dying the thread of this dance?

We dabble in code. And now,
having a feeble mind of its own,
the machine has arrived, GMOs.
Do not salute; meet your new suit.
Take it out for a fit and a spin; sex and food
are merely what we make them,
and life, that risen urge, wakes
each morning to solve its own problem.

I know the sadness of leaving home.
Every time I've turned, another forest
has fallen, another form named and extinguished.
Those dolphins were my friends too.
I do not mean to hold you back
with nostalgia, but I am bewildered
at their lack of amazement and wonder.
How do they make it without thank-you?
Even as a child I knew his tears
were not for himself.

I drink the newly rinsed rain
and hold the rolling sky as a lover.
I know the cloth of it.
My naked body is the first fern on settled crust;
my mind the math of galactic regeneration.
I'm too busy dying for death.

I am Prepared

I am prepared by the slow pull
    of fast talkers, by poverty
    and the repetition of acid rain.
I am prepared by the accountant
    and medical examiner.
I am prepared in the gauze
    and bubble wrap
    of dumbed down news casting,
    in the asphalt libraries and
    smoky casinos of this hard town.
I am prepared to die.

I am prepared by the onslaught of ownership
    and the overload of naming and meaning.
I am prepared by removing my name.
I am prepared by darkness.
I am prepared by a circle of men singing underground,
    by the curve of her that defies
    the straight line and metaphor mind.
I am prepared by snow.

I am prepared by the voyagers with DNA,
    by memory and longing.
I am prepared by the ceaseless sea.
I am prepared by fasting, by
    the morning of my wedding.
I am prepared by the side of the road.
I am prepared to lead again.
I am prepared for another star.

I am prepared by the smell of flowers
    after each round of dancing.
I am prepared by the dew
    between your thighs, but first
    the welcome of your soft words.
I am prepared by the butterfly teasing of us.
I am prepared to fly.

Your Red Shirt

Though I sometimes see you
(or don't see you)
as a ghost, I sing to you.
I sing to you as a stranger,
or strange wanderer, stepping
over fallen logs, crossing the stream
to walk beside me then disappearing
into an adjacent ravine. Gone
for days it seems—I sing to you.

I sing to you now though
I have brushed you like a fly
or tried to ditch you
by making a sudden turn
at the rusted refrigerator half sunk
in silky mud. I turned off
three days back, and now I hear
the echoic snap of a twig,
ravens charging ahead of the bear.

Was that lens flare, lightning,
or the flash of your red shirt?
You seem more scout than threat.
Today I find it false
to say that I am alone.
Today, I sing to you.

She wakes to record the poem she wrote
so vivid in her dream, reaches

for journal and pen—nothing translates.
In the sleep-space she was
constructing with pieces
of floating metal, not language.
Our song like that too.

What you make from the sky
above the rolling green and sacred stones
knows my higher mind.
Are those your designs
in the twisted wheat and geometric rye?
You visit me there.

Birds are sexing in the sycamore
for all to see.
My lover is not far. I sing
to her companion as well,
to the wanderer of her.
We are made again and again.

One day you send a postcard
from Tennessee or Tralfamadore.
You look different
but I know you just the same.
Old friend, hear me sing. This time
I walk toward you,
the patterns of us
coming through my hands.

Found on a Rock

Those of us under contract to write
of the Great Moving Mystery
as it flows out upon
the elevations of earth's plane
must often work alone.

Sometimes a trail forged by the Sherwa;
sometimes this floundering in waist high snow.

The mountain on my left, then
the mountain on my right—one thing
does not necessarily lead to another
as the inhabitants here believe.
The children are given straight lines
with which to play
and taught a curious form called *ownership*.

At a camp near the edge
of a great city I misplace my notes,
succumb to a local condition known as loss.
I am given a cup of Temporary
by a singer on the road
and understanding is restored.

Of course, there are obstacles.
Cannibalism is at the core
of human expansion and tied directly

to that runaway code
we've been commissioned to observe.

I leave small stacks of stones
on rounded hills as encouragement.
These beacons are linked.
When this planet is in retrograde
there is shelter below the beams.
Our paths will surely cross.

PERFECT IDEA OF OCEAN

You're expectant, wanting
the sun to burst inside your name.
A flaming boxcar used to do,
one high voltage love after another.
Your brand of stopping is slowing down, just

enough to move through it.
There'll be time to halt up ahead, you say.
You've passed those moments
like so many wild onions or clumps
of rain grass—it can wait.

I am the paintbrush of the optimist,
the inevitable obliterating sunrise.
I think I can afford another story,
and then another; just one more town to build
then destroy in the dirt before dinner,

one more cloud to explode.
But sunrise is not a pinhead
or a switch—as above, so below.
The story of finally finding her or
a thousand roses delivered

gets washed further from shore.
Perhaps you are the perfect idea of ocean,
anticipation a wave curling
over on itself. You can't remember
when this wasn't going on?

WHAT SHOULD NOT BE TAKEN
at the pueblo feast days

Where do your eyes go
when you dance, when you dance,
when your feet become
the north and south of the sun?

Do you look at them; do you look
to the sky, to the earth,
to that place beyond, to no place?
Pardon my too many questions.
I was once a stable hand
in the empire of this wrecking.

I don't even know those people
whose names they drop in the news,
but I hear them growling
in droves and in drones.
Where do *your* eyes go?

Across the summer of retreated grass
you ankle bells and beaded shield.
Across the open sky the tremble
of the danced up earth.
    A medicine bird from the west.
I, too, will avert my eyes.
It is not polite to steal.

SEARCHLESS

This morning's sun
did not rise, did not enter,
did not strike the stuccoed wall.
This morning's sun is bright
and without name.

There's an assumption that I have
seen the world for what it is.
I bandy these words about:
neutrino, quasar, Sub Sahara.
And also these: dismantle, deconstruct.
I have to walk away.

A light through the window
has found me, though
I can't say if it was searching.
But something other than me
was doing all that looking, and now
the kitchen has shifted.

A flapping and flashing in the leaves—
perhaps pigeons practicing with knives,
or a Cooper's Hawk pulling
entrails from a mouse. Perhaps
the next universe looking in.
Is there anything here
that isn't moving?

Everything Touches

The wind teases a cluster of finger-thin leaves.
A pine chair touches the floor. The music comes through.

We go out to pink clouds with purple smudges.
We talk with one another under the words.

Mud houses snuggly the children; a laugh circles the world.
The truth in which we join is undefined—all is well.

You squat before the fire, look into her eyes. The river
bends and bends and bends. It all happens in a nod.

www.ingramcontent.com/pod-product-compliance
Lightning Source LLC
Chambersburg PA
CBHW051839040426
42447CB00006B/614